LIFE EDUCATION

Look Good, Feel Good

Written by Liz Swinden
Illustrated by Kevin Faerber

FRANKLIN WATTS

A Division of Grolier Publishing

NEW YORK • LONDON • HONG KONG • SYDNEY
DANBURY, CONNECTICUT

First American Edition 1997 by
Franklin Watts
A Division of Grolier Publishing
Sherman Turnpike
Danbury, CT 06816

10 9 8 7 6 5 4 3 2 1
Swinden, Liz.
    Look good, feel good / Liz Swinden.
        p. cm. — (Life education)
    Includes index.
    ISBN 0-531-14428-3
    1. Children—Health and hygiene—Juvenile
    literature.
    [1. Health.] I. Title. II. Series.
    RA777.S95 1997
    613—dc20   96-11727
                                    CIP AC
Printed in Italy

Edited by: Helen Lanz
Designed by: Sally Boothroyd
Commissioned photography by:
Peter Millard
Illustrations by: Kevin Faerber
Medical consultant: Dr. Michael
Redfern

Acknowledgments:
Commissioned photography by Peter Millard:
cover; title page.
Researched photography: Bubbles 11
(I. West); Franklin Watts CD transparency;
John Walmsley 13; Robert Harding 9
(C. Gilnane/Burda, Gmbh), 17 (R. Cundy), 27
(F. Hache); The Hutchinson Library 14, 18
(D. Hodge), 22; Science Photo Library 4, 24 (A.
Hart-Davis), 25 (G. Tompkinson); Zefa 6
(Koenig), 15, 21.
Artwork: Cartoon illustrations by Kevin
Faerber throughout.

The publishers wish to acknowledge that the
photographs reproduced in this book have
been posed by models or obtained from
photographic picture agencies.

Franklin Watts and Life Education
International are indebted to Susan Kaplin,
Amanda Friend, Vince Hatton, and Laurie
Noffs for their invaluable help.

Franklin Watts would like to extend their
special thanks to all the actors who appear in
the Life Education books (Key Stage 3):

Hester Cann   Chloe Parsons
James Ceppi di Lecco   Dipali Patel
James Chandler

"*Each second we live is a new and unique moment of the universe, a moment
that will never be again...And what do we teach our children? We teach
them that two and two make four and that Paris is the capital of France.*

*When will we also teach them: do you know who you are? You are a marvel.
You are unique. In all the years that have passed, there has never been
another child like you. And look at your body – what a wonder it is! Your
legs, your arms, your clever fingers, the way you move. You may become a
Shakespeare, a Michelangelo, a Beethoven. You have the capacity for
anything. Yes, you are a marvel. And when you grow up, can you then harm
another who is, like you, a marvel? You must cherish one another. You must
work – we must all work – to make this world worthy of its children.*"

Pablo Casals

A famous Spanish musician, also noted for his humanitarian beliefs.
(1876 - 1973)

CONTENTS

Get ready to
use your brains
and expand your
minds. We're going to
look at YOU in the world.

A GOOD PERFORMANCE

You don't have to have just stepped off a stage set or out of a Hollywood movie to look and feel good! Looking and feeling good is about far more than that. It's about YOU. It's about knowing that you're important, valuing yourself. After all, you deserve to give yourself the best, don't you?

IT'S UP TO YOU

As you become more independent, you will be taking on more responsibility for looking after yourself. As an adult, it'll be totally up to you what you eat, drink, and wear, what exercise you do and what lifestyle you lead. Are you ready for this?

SOLID FUEL

OK, so you know what you like to eat. Maybe it's fried chicken or chocolate ice cream or stir-fried vegetables and rice. Common sense will tell you something about food, but there are some basic facts that are really helpful to know if you want your body to perform well.

You're at the stage of your life when your body is developing and growing very fast, so you need to have a range of different types of food to provide energy and keep you going. Your body needs a balance of carbohydrates, some protein, some fat, some vitamins and minerals, and some fiber every day. These might not sound very appetizing, but you can't help but eat from these food categories every time you take a mouthful of something!

This photograph shows glycoprotein fibers in the body and was magnified to over 12,300 times to make them visible on a 35mm photographic slide.

FINGER ON THE PULSE

Most of your energy comes from carbohydrates in the form of either starches or sugars. Starches are in foods such as bread, rice, pasta, and potatoes, while there is a lot of sugar in processed foods like cakes, cookies, candy, and ice cream. Sugar does provide energy, but nothing else, and it's bad for your teeth.

Fiber is a type of carbohydrate needed by your body to help your intestines digest your food more efficiently. It's found in a variety of foods including fruit, vegetables, whole wheat bread, whole grains, beans, legumes, and nuts.

ROOM FOR GROWTH

Protein is used by the body for growth and repair. It's found in foods like meat, fish, cheese, eggs, milk, nuts, and beans.

BEWARE OF THE OIL WELL!

There are two main types of fat. Foods containing saturated fats include butter, milk, cheese, and meats as well as some vegetable oils (including coconut or palm oil) and processed foods like cakes and cookies. Unsaturated fats are found in vegetable oils such as soya and sunflower, oily fish, and some nuts. Fats have double the calories of carbohydrates and proteins. Saturated fats can raise the level of cholesterol in the blood. A high level of cholesterol is associated with a greater risk of heart disease. Unsaturated fats don't have this effect, so to lessen the risk of heart disease it's a good idea to use the unsaturated fats and to cut down on cholesterol-rich foods such as eggs, butter, and ice cream. Food contains calories which are a measure of the energy they provide.

While it's useful to know about how many calories there are in different foods, beware of getting hung up on counting calories.

orange = 30 cals

chocolate cookie = 150 cals

sausage = 250 cals

peanut butter sandwich = 300 cals

Ooh I can't possibly have that – it's got 300 calories.

Boring...

MINING FOR MINERALS

Contrary to what the pharmaceutical companies say, vitamins and minerals aren't just found in bottles in pharmacies and health food stores! They're found in a wide range of foods, and we need small amounts of about 15 different vitamins and 20 minerals to enable essential chemical processes to happen in our bodies.

AVAILABLE IN ALL SIZES

Everyone requires different amounts of food, and this will vary at different stages of your life. When you're going through puberty and growing fast, you probably need to eat as much as an adult. Extra fat gets stored under the skin, however, so if you eat too much fat and don't exercise enough, you may be carrying around excess weight. But remember that we all come in a variety of shapes and sizes, so it's not always helpful to talk about ideal weights.

Different people process food at different rates, so there's no hard and fast rule about exactly how much you should eat – however, ensuring a good balance of foods is a good idea.

5

FIVE-STAR FUEL

If you want to look and feel good, then eating healthily is a vital step on the way. Knowing about protein, carbohydrates, fats, and sugar is useful, but it's important to know about what's in the foods you like to eat so that you can see if you're getting a good balance of all the nutrients you need. A healthy diet means eating plenty of fiber foods with a smaller proportion of protein and fats.

It's useful to know what the foods you eat are high, medium, or low in.

ENERGY OR CALORIES

Your body needs fuel to function properly, whether you're walking, running, or sleeping. Energy comes from the body's fuel – fats, carbohydrates, and proteins in food, but the amount you need depends on your age, how active you are, and your metabolism. The metabolism regulates how the body turns food into energy, and it varies greatly between individuals. Your metabolism changes, especially as you get older, which is why many older people are heavier than when they were young. If you eat too many calories, they get stored as fat.

A particular food isn't bad for you just because it may be high in calories. It all depends how much you eat and how often you eat it. Calories in themselves are not the enemy!

FAT-ATTACK

It's generally acknowledged that high fat consumption is associated with heart attacks and with being overweight. Fat has more calories than the equivalent amount of protein or sugar. The *type* of fat you eat is important, too. It's much healthier to eat low or unsaturated fats, such as vegetable oils and fats in fish, than saturated ones, such as those in dairy products and meat.

SUGAR IS SWEET

Many people in the western world have far too much sugar in their diets. This is because sugar-rich foods like candy and soft drinks taste good and are popular. Also, manufactured foods like cakes, jams, cookies, cereals, and pies contain surprisingly high amounts of sugar.

Sugar is also a major factor in tooth decay, and it provides "empty" calories with few extra nutrients.

SPARE THE SALT

You only need up to one gram of salt each day, yet many people eat between three and eight grams daily by adding it to food before and after cooking, purely out of habit. There's also "hidden" salt in many manufactured goods like canned soups, cereals, and pies. There is believed to be a link between high blood pressure and high salt consumption. Research with people who already have high blood pressure shows that taking in extra salt can actually make their condition worse.

FOOD AND FIBER

You can get a good amount of fiber by eating cereals that have "added fiber" or you could increase your intake of fresh fruit and vegetables, which are a good source of natural fiber.

WHAT'S IN THESE FOODS?

Which of these foods do you think have the highest fat, sugar, and salt content? Which have the highest amounts of fiber?

Is your body getting all the different nutrients that it needs?

YOU ARE WHAT YOU EAT?

Deciding what you eat may seem like a rather small decision, but it's actually an important one as it influences your health, growth, and development. The decisions you make about your lifestyle become lifestyle habits – in this case, your eating habits. If you get into the habit of eating a snack when you get in from school, your body comes to expect this. It's easy to see how such habits are formed.

JUST ONE CORNETTO

Forming habits is no bad thing, but what if the snack was a huge bowl of delicious ice cream, topped with some cookies, topped with a whirl of fresh cream, topped with some grated chocolate, topped with... How many of these could your body (and teeth) take before it started to become a problem? You'd have to do an awful lot of exercise to balance the calories!

CASE STUDY 1:

Charlie is 14. He attends school but doesn't like or take part in any of the sports offered there. In his spare time he watches a lot of TV and videos and sometimes helps his dad with home repairs and carpentry. This is what Charlie ate one day last week:

Like many lifestyle choices, it's probably easier to get into good habits from the start than it is to try and break habits that are not good for you or your body. This doesn't mean to say that ice cream topped with just about everything isn't OK – once in a while though!

Tuesday 12th February

Breakfast Bowl of cereal, milk, sugar. Orange juice.

Mid-morning – Bar of chocolate, can of soda orange.

Lunch at school – Pizza, fries, carton of milk, doughnut.

After school – Bag of chips, can of cola.

Dinner – Meatballs in tomato sauce, pasta, carrots, fruit salad, and ice cream. Iced tea with sugar.

CASE STUDY 2:

Dina is also 14. She is a member of the local athletic club and trains three times a week and on Saturdays. She's trying to keep her weight down. This is a fairly typical day's eating for Dina:

Tuesday 12th February

Breakfast – Granola, fruit, and black coffee.

Lunch – Rice cakes, cottage cheese, an orange, water.

After school – Diet cola.

Dinner – Low-calorie ready meal (eg. pasta and sauce) with salad.

Do you think that if Charlie and Dina eat these kind of foods every day they are both getting a balanced diet? What advice would you give each of them?

Neither Charlie nor Dina eats a balanced diet. Charlie is eating too much fat, sugar, and salt and not enough fiber. He needs to cut down on these and eat more fruit and vegetables. Dina's diet is better than Charlie's but she is probably not eating enough calories. In relation to the amount of exercise she is doing she could probably eat more – especially protein foods – and not put on weight.

Many adults consume one or two glasses of wine with an evening meal. Drinking in this way once in a while is fine but excess alcohol over a long period can result in effects such as liver damage and stomach ulcers.

"You can't be too rich or too thin." Duchess of Windsor, wife of King Edward VIII, 1896 – 1986

What do you think of this statement?

A FASHION TO FOLLOW?

The idea of what is fashionable is different depending on the society in which you live. Since the 1960s, western societies have been bombarded with media images of what is believed to be the perfect female figure. Fashion models have been presented as the ideal, so the pressure to be slim is intense, particularly for women. Unfortunately, eating disorders, such as anorexia nervosa and bulimia are now a major health problem. There is an abnormal fear of gaining weight and so a starvation regime is embarked on, which can lead to severe health problems or even death. It's vital that people at risk of developing these problems are identified and supported early on. We all have to decide what "looking good and feeling good" means for us, because it's clear that (for some people) it can involve taking too many risks!

LOOKS GOOD, TASTES GOOD!

Once you've got a basic knowledge of food and nutrition, it's time to start getting more involved in preparing your own food. After all, you know what you like – why leave it to others? It's good to be able to feed yourself well – not just because it makes you more independent, but because you can invite your friends over!

COOK UP A STORM

Feeding yourself and other people can be one of the most enjoyable and sociable things anyone can do. You don't have to take cooking lessons or follow complicated recipes, either. You can often pick up ideas when you are out shopping – just wandering around a supermarket for example. Maybe one of the many cooking programs on television will get you started. Or if you know someone who's a really good cook, you could ask them to show you some easy dishes. Prepare your taste buds for a treat!

Take care! If you aren't used to using the oven, ask for help before you embark on your cooking crusade!

"A good cook is like a sorceress who dispenses happiness."
Elsa Schiaparelli, Italian fashion designer, 1890 – 1973

SOME IDEAS FOR YOU TO TRY...

Things on toast or bread
These are really quick-to-make, nutritious snack meals, especially if you use whole wheat bread and cut down on the butter or use a low-fat spread. On top you could have baked beans, which are high in fiber, or scrambled eggs, or mushrooms. Be sure to grill instead of fry, and use low-fat cheese or slice it very thinly!

To scramble an egg you'll need: 1 egg, 1tbsp of margarine, pepper to taste.

Beat the egg in a bowl and add some pepper. Melt the margarine in a saucepan over a medium to high heat. Add the egg and stir constantly with a wooden spoon to prevent it from sticking to the pan. When the egg has formed a mass, remove from the heat, put on the ready-made toast and eat.

Stuffed potatoes

Quick if you've got a microwave – or can take up to an hour in a conventional oven. These are high in fiber, especially if you eat the skins too. You can use lots of different fillings – cottage cheese, baked beans, coleslaw, broccoli, yogurt with spring onion or chives.

Take a medium-sized potato and wash and puncture two or three times to break the skin (this will prevent the potato from exploding in the oven). Put into a microwave for between 5 and 7 minutes, depending on the size of the potato, or put into a preheated conventional oven (set at 350° F/180° C) for up to an hour. Keep checking the potato – when a fork goes in easily, it is done.

Stir-fried vegetables

Take a selection of your favorite vegetables – onions, mushrooms, peppers, cabbage, zucchini, carrots, celery — and chop into small chunks or thin slices. Put a tablespoon of cooking oil into a wok or large frying pan and heat until smoking. Add the vegetables, keeping those that cook quickly (like mushrooms) until last. Keeping the heat fairly high, stir the vegetables around the pan. Keep stirring for 3–4 minutes, then taste for crunchiness. Serve with bread, pasta, or rice, adding some low-salt soy sauce to taste.

DRINK TO YOUR HEALTH!

Your body needs plenty of fluid throughout the day. Water is the cheapest and easiest thing to drink, but many people prefer other drinks too. Tea and coffee both contain caffeine, a drug that stimulates the nervous system, so it's a good idea not to have more than two cups a day. Soft drinks are often high in sugar and caffeine, although there are sugar-free and caffeine-free versions. Stick to water, bottled water, or fruit juice, and you won't go wrong.

It's a good idea to prepare your ingredients before you start to cook.

MUSCLING IN

Looking good and feeling good aren't just about healthy eating. Your body also needs to be exercised regularly, so that the muscles stay in good condition and your body systems, such as your circulatory system, are kept in tip-top working order. Exercising regularly makes our bodies more efficient. If you've ever had an arm or leg in a cast, you'll know how weak and feeble it looks when the cast comes off.

INSURANCE POLICY

Regular exercise is also like an insurance policy. If you keep yourself reasonably fit throughout your youth and as you get older, your body is more able to repair itself, fight off infections, and so on. Osteoporosis is a disease that affects people in later life. The bones become weak and brittle, which can result in fractures and loss of height. Building up your bone mass through regular exercise is recognized as being a way of preventing this disease.

BUT I HATE SPORTS!

Exercising your body doesn't mean you have to become athletic and take up competitive sports, although many people do because they enjoy it. Some people are put off sports while at school because they feel self-conscious about their bodies, or because they don't feel very skilled at the particular activities, or simply because they don't enjoy it. Find the level of involvement that's right for you. Another important aspect is enjoyment – it's no good doing exercise that you hate! If it's something you like, you'll enjoy keeping it up.

Running, walking, and swimming are particularly good exercise, because they use most of the muscles in the body. They're also cheap to do and don't require any elaborate or costly equipment.

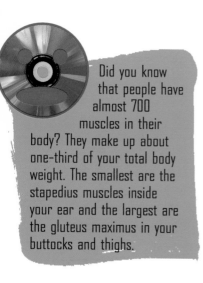

Did you know that people have almost 700 muscles in their body? They make up about one-third of your total body weight. The smallest are the stapedius muscles inside your ear and the largest are the gluteus maximus in your buttocks and thighs.

AND STRETCH AND BEND...

Aerobics has been popular for some years, but what exactly is aerobic activity? Well, it's activity that increases the body's ability to get oxygen circulating around it more efficiently. To do this, the activity needs to be strenuous but not exhausting and to go on for at least 20 minutes at a time so that the heart and lungs work harder. Cycling, running, and swimming can all be aerobic, but things like squash or weight-lifting aren't because they involve bursts of activity.

WARM UP, WIND DOWN

With any activity, it's always important to be sure to warm up and cool down properly by stretching and moving gently. It can be too stressful for your body to go from "rest", or non-exercise, to suddenly performing continuous exercise. Similarly, it's important to cool down, to return your heartbeat from a raised level during exercise to your standard heartbeat pattern.

Exercising two or three times a week, for a period of about half an hour at a time, can help to keep you healthy and fit.

PROBLEM PAGE

MISERABLE MIRIAM

Dear Aunty Sue,
I hate sports at school because I'm a bit chubby and the other girls in my class all look great in their shorts, and I just feel terrible. I'm always making excuses so I don't have to change clothes, and I think the teacher will catch on soon and I'll get into trouble. I'd like to be more active, but what can I do?

Miriam

Dear Miriam,
First of all, don't worry. Yours is a more common problem than you think. Some of those girls who you say "look great in their shorts" are probably just as self-conscious as you. Is your teacher someone you could talk to? She might have some useful suggestions.

Have you a friend in class who you can talk to about this? See if she feels the same as you. Maybe you can go to a gym together after school hours where you can start to seriously tone up your body. Then you will feel less self-conscious when you participate at school. Not only can exercise be fun, but regular exercise will make you feel more in control of your life, too.

Aunty Sue

BREATHE DEEP

It's quite possible that you take your lungs for granted. After all, breathing is what human beings do – isn't it? Looking after your lungs is just another part of the process of keeping your body working properly. Your lungs are designed to absorb oxygen from the air into your body so that your blood can take up the oxygen and deliver it all around the body. Regular exercise helps the body to be more efficient at this, but your lungs need to be kept free of pollution to do their job properly.

Did you know that in a day, an adult breathes enough air to fill 1,000 party balloons? Babies take up to 60 breaths a minute, while adults take up to 18.

The Quechua people who live 12,000 feet up in the Andes Mountains of South America have larger lungs and hearts than normal to carry more oxygen. This is because the higher up you go, the less dense the air is. This means that there is less oxygen in the air. As a result, the Quechua people need to breathe in a larger amount of air in order to extract the oxygen that the body needs. Their hearts need to pump the blood to the lungs more often, in order for enough oxygen to be absorbed and carried around their bodies. Sounds exhausting, doesn't it?

MUTUAL ATTRACTION?

There are many forms of air pollution in today's society, but there's also an individual pollution kit. Despite the fact that smoking is linked to lung cancer and heart disease, this doesn't seem to stop some people from doing it. Telling a young person that they are likely to die from a smoking-related disease in middle age may not mean much, but there are other, more persuasive reasons for them to stop.

"Non-smoking should be regarded as the normal social behavior." World Health Organization, 1979

D'you think those boys will be here again?

They should be. Dean said they usually come on Fridays.

Those girls are here again... You know the red-haired girl you danced with last week? I think she really likes you...

Too bad. She's really good-looking, but she smells of cigarette smoke. You know I hate that.

Why doesn't he come over? They've been here for ages, but he looks like he's avoiding me.

Look, his friend's gone to buy more drinks. I'll go over and see what's happening.

What's the matter with your friend?

What d'you mean?

Er... actually Dean hates cigarette smoke. He's really into fitness... training for the soccer team and all that.

Carol thinks he's really nice and she was hoping they'd get together tonight.

YOUR HABIT – OR MINE?

Some people choose not to smoke – but when they go out to enjoy an evening with friends, they may find themselves inhaling other people's cigarette smoke. Passive smoking, or secondary smoking, exposes people to the same health risks, although at a slightly reduced level, as the smoker.

Let's get this straight – there are the smokers who have chosen to take the health risks associated with smoking, and there are the nonsmokers who have decided they don't want those health risks. Yet they're being exposed to the risks anyway. Can you think of a way around this problem?

THE AIR WE BREATHE...

Of course, there's a limit to how much we can affect the quality of the air we breathe in every day, especially in city areas where the air pollution is greater... or is there? You could look into doing a project at school to measure the amount of pollutants in the air in your district and then publicize the results through the local paper.

Would you like a cigarette?

No thanks – I've already had one!

15

SQUEAKY CLEAN

Yes, you've probably heard the joke about skin being the thing that stops everything else from falling out, but it's a lot more than that. It provides protection for what's inside; it stops germs from invading our bodies; it makes vitamin D; it allows the body to control its temperature by allowing moisture (sweat) to escape; and it contains part of our sense of touch.

> The film had hardly started when his arm crept round me, and then...

> Then what?

> Then there was this awful smell and I knew...

> Knew what?

> I knew that Dave and I were destined never to go out with each other again. Embarrassing or what?

IT'S ONLY NATURAL

As you get older, and especially as you reach adolescence, your sweat glands start working more and so your smell changes.

Did you know that every day, your body loses about a cup of moisture through sweating? That's the same as a glass of orange juice.

It's a natural part of growing up. So if you want to be "nice to be near," you'll need to watch your washing habits. A daily bath or shower will help get rid of sweat, dirt, and dead skin, or a thorough all-over wash is just as good. Sweat glands are most numerous under your arms and around your genitals, although feet need regular attention, too.

HELLO SUNSHINE...?

Getting a suntan used to be everyone's idea of what to do on your vacations – but no more. Overexposure to the sun increases the risk of skin cancer and also prematurely ages the skin. If you're out in the sun, wherever you live, cover up with a hat and long sleeves and use sunscreen on any exposed parts.

CRYSTAL CLEAR

Just as your sweat glands start working overtime, so do the small glands just below the skin surface which produce sebum. This is an oily fluid that keeps the skin smooth and the hair shiny, but some people – especially teenagers – produce too much, causing blemishes to occur.

Blemishes will mostly clear up on their own and there's no proof that expensive creams are any better than soap and water. If you have bad acne, however, it can leave scars, so do go to your doctor, who can help. A healthy diet may help reduce blemishes too.

"DOWN BELOW"

Like the rest of your body, your genital area needs washing every day. Fluids such as urine, menstrual blood, vaginal fluid, and semen are all clean but, having left the body, can be places for bacteria to breed – so washing is particularly important. (Regularly changing and washing your underwear is important too).

Girls need to be careful to wash and dry the genital area from front to back so that bacteria from the rectum doesn't get into the vagina or urethra. Boys, if uncircumcised, should roll back their foreskin and wash underneath. Using deodorants or antiperspirants in this area isn't a good idea, as they will irritate the skin – and make your eyes water!

KEEP YOUR HAIR ON!

As if growing, sweating more, and getting blemishes isn't enough, adolescents also get more hair – under their arms, on their arms and legs and faces (especially boys), and around the genitals. Hair traps odors, dirt and bacteria, and needs to be washed frequently. For most people there is a choice about shaving off the hair. Girls can choose whether to shave their legs and under their arms; boys can choose whether to shave their facial hair.

ALL STRESSED UP AND NOWHERE TO GO

S tress is part of life; it always has been. Ever since prehistoric man worried about whether he'd find a woolly mammoth to kill and take back to feed his tribe, human beings have lived with a huge range of pressures and strains. What experts agree on, though, is that we're all under more stress in present-day society than ever before and we all need to find ways of coping with it if we're to stay looking and feeling good.

I hope there's going to be enough to go around...

STRESS FACTORS

It's well known that certain life events cause greater amounts of stress than others. If any of the following have happened to you or those close to you recently, chances are that you're under abnormal stress:

Physical changes
Divorce or separation
Prison
Personal illness or injury
Marriage
Being fired or other problems
   at work
Pregnancy
Change in family's finances
Coping with holidays
Death of close friend
Starting new job or school
Moving
Changes at school
   (e.g., exams)
Change in sleeping habits
Taking on new responsibilities
Death in the family

REALLY, I'M FINE!

Some people are better at coping with stress than others – they seem to just sail through life – easygoing and relaxed. Then there are others who always seem anxious. Most people are probably somewhere in between.

When you're under a lot of stress, you can suffer from minor disorders such as headaches, indigestion, or sleeplessness, but there's increasing evidence to show that more serious conditions such as asthma, ulcers, high blood pressure (hypertension), and heart disease are linked to high stress levels, too.

SIGNS AND SYMPTOMS

Stress shows itself in different ways and it's good to be able to recognize some of them.

- cold, sweaty hands
- loss of or increase in weight
- skin problems
- outbursts of temper
- panic attacks
- exaggerating problems

- feeling tense or helpless
- fidgeting
- eating more
- drinking too much
- poor concentration
- stomach upsets

And you can probably think of more!

WHERE IS YOUR STRESS COMING FROM?

1 What's causing Calvin stress right now?
Answer: He's got important exams coming up in two months, and he is worried he won't do well. He isn't sleeping properly.

2 What's the setting for this?
Answer: School (he's weak in a couple of subjects and is struggling to keep up) and home (his dad is really pushing him to succeed).

3 Can he do anything about it?
Answer: Calvin thinks he'll just put it out of his mind and hope everything works out OK.

4 What choices does Calvin have to get help?
Answer: Persuade his mom to talk to his dad about lessening the pressure / talk to his teacher at school about getting extra help / get support from friends in the same situation / find ways to relax (e.g., sports, relaxation techniques).

RELAX!!!

Regular relaxation is very important in dealing with the stresses of life. Finding out what relaxes you is important – maybe it's listening to music or playing your own, playing sports, or learning techniques for relaxation or meditation. At the very least, soaking in a hot bubble bath is worth a try!

Remember, suffering from stress isn't a sign of weakness. We all suffer from it one way or another, but getting help and finding out how to cope is a sign of strength! Don't just put up with it as part of life – you can do something to lessen the stress!

THE "FEEL GOOD" FACTOR

Making sure your body is properly cared for is only half the story. Health is holistic – about the whole person. Feeling good and looking good are about your thoughts and feelings – how you feel about yourself and your relationships with other people and your place in the world. It's said that if you feel good about yourself, then you'll be more likely to get along with others, care for yourself, and stay healthy. Feeling good about yourself is sometimes called having good self-esteem.

FEELING THE BLUES

There are times when we all feel rotten, thinking no one loves us and we just want to crawl into a corner and have a good cry. It's strange, but humans seem to have the ability to hang on to all the bad things people say to us and then when we feel low, something triggers all those bad things from the past and we end up in a vicious circle of self-doubt and negative feelings. But if we're aware of this happening, there are things we can do to start feeling better about ourselves.

Ask almost anyone to make two lists – things they like and don't like about themselves – and it's pretty certain that the second list will be a lot longer than the first!

THINGS I LIKE
my feet are Ok
generous
keep clean

THINGS I DON'T LIKE
big bottom
no good at math
rotten at sports
blemishes
bite my nails
can't sing
always forgetting things

An important aspect of feeling good about yourself is knowing what you believe in and being able to stick to it. The more confident you are in yourself, the more you'll be able to hold on to your own views and not be influenced too much by those around you. Resisting peer pressure isn't always easy though.

If you try this, see that you make the first list at least as long as the second one!

It's important to have faith in yourself – if you believe in yourself, others will, too.

"And above all things, never think that you're not good enough yourself. A [person] should never think that. My belief is that in life people will take you very much at your own reckoning." from *The Small House at Allington* by Anthony Trollope, English novelist (1815 – 1882)

It's Friday. Let's all go to my house. My parents won't be home till late and there are some cigarettes my sister brought home from college.

Ok.

Great.

Why don't we get some beer from the supermarket?

I'm not really into all that. Why don't we go to the library and get some of our homework out of the way so we can enjoy the rest of the weekend?

Yuck.

Spoil sport.

Why don't you get a life?

Oh come on, we can do all that work on Sunday at my house. Just come for a bit?

SHOULD I?

Solving dilemmas and making good decisions isn't easy, but as with everything, there's always a way forward. Here are some useful tips that can really help you make up your mind.

✓ Be as clear as you can about what the problem is or what the choices are.

✓ Writing it down often helps.

✓ Make a list of the options open to you.

✓ If it's a choice between two things, make a list of pros and cons for each one.

✓ Have you got all the information you need to decide?

✓ Do you need to check anything out with your friends or family?

✓ Assess the outcomes: what will happen if you decide to do "x" or "y"?

LOOKING DREADFUL, FEELING ROTTEN

We all get sick from time to time. Most illnesses are caused directly by infections that are the result of germs of various kinds such as viruses and bacteria entering the body. Sometimes the body behaves as if it is being infected when it is not, for example when it has an allergic reaction like hay fever. Much less common are illnesses in which some of the cells malfunction, such as cancer where the affected cells multiply uncontrollably, or diabetes, where cells stop making insulin. The cause of these kinds of condition are complex but can involve our lifestyle.

ON THE ALERT

Your body is always on the alert for any infections. It has its own complex self-care mechanism, or immune system, made up of cells and chemicals that monitor us constantly for invasions of unwanted bacteria or viruses.

We develop antibodies, manufactured by the white blood cells, or lymphocytes. These are activated when a germ enters the body. The lymphocytes analyze the invader, forming an anti-body that attacks and kills it.

The body then stores the information so that if a similar germ returns, the body is ready to deal with it. This way, immunity to specific infections can be maintained by each individual.

The rise in travel has resulted in the spread of disease and increased the need for vaccination programs.

Edward Jenner discovered vaccination in 1796 when he used the vaccinia virus to protect against smallpox. Vaccines are produced by artificially cultivating the bacteria that cause illness. After being specially treated in a laboratory to become weakened, they are then injected into the body, inducing the blood to form antibodies to fight the disease.

FACE IT!

Perhaps the most obvious sign of the body's immune system is the formation of pus, the white stuff in a blemish or pimple. Made up of dead cells and microbes, the body usually removes the material by itself and stops the infection from spreading. If for some reason your immune system isn't working properly, the blemish may need some help to disappear. Keep your skin clean and use antiseptic products as needed.

GETTING BETTER?

If an infection doesn't heal by itself, bacterial or fungal diseases can usually – but not in every case – be treated with antibiotic drugs. While some medicinal drugs can help the body's own immune system, taking drugs that are not designed for this purpose, or not using medicinal drugs properly, can actually severely hinder the body's own healing processes.

The body's immune system becomes less efficient if we continually undermine it. It's easy to abuse our bodies – we might choose to eat a poor diet or never exercise. Some people contaminate their bodies through abusing alcohol or other drugs, by smoking cigarettes, or by not getting enough sleep. When the body is run down, you become more vulnerable to infection and disease.

SWEET DREAMS

Sleep is when the body has time to relax and repair itself. During puberty, you are growing fast and using a lot of energy so you need plenty of sleep. Fourteen- to eighteen-year-olds probably need around 8 – 9 hours sleep every night, but it varies from person to person. During sleep, everyone has about five dreams every night, although many of us do not remember what we dream.

It's not fully understood why we dream, although it's recognized as being linked with the unconscious part of ourselves. Dreams may go over events of the day or highlight our anxieties. There are many different theories about the meaning of dreams.

Dreams such as this one often indicate fear or the presence of danger in someone's life.

GETTING THE MESSAGE ACROSS

Drugs are substances that affect the way the body and mind work. They can increase, reduce, or block the action of the natural chemicals in the body and, as such, should only be used with extreme caution. Some are made from plants while others are made synthetically from chemicals. Different types of drugs fall into a variety of categories, but basically they can be classed in two main groups: medicines/prescribed drugs and illegal drugs

MEDICINAL PURPOSES

Most of us take medicines of one sort or another from time to time, such as aspirin when we've got a headache. This is a medicinal type of drug, used to relieve pain.

Medical drugs work in many different ways. Some are used to boost the levels of the body's natural chemicals that may be in short supply, such as in the case of people with diabetes who can't produce the hormone insulin. Other drugs, such as antibiotics, can be introduced to the body to help the body's own immune system fight against an invading bacteria.

It's important to take medicines only as prescribed, and also only by the person they are prescribed for.

A STATE OF CONFUSION

There are some medical drugs that deliberately set out to confuse the body. The contraceptive pill rearranges the female hormonal balance each month, preventing the ovary from releasing an egg and making the womb hostile to sperm, and so preventing conception.

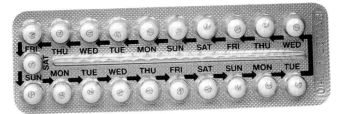

THE RISK FACTOR

While medicines are prescribed for the purpose of returning the body to health, or trying to correct chemical imbalances, there is always an element of risk in introducing foreign substances to the body. Although the drug may perform its intended function, there can be "side effects." These are reactions the drug actually causes in the body.

BRIDGING THE GAP

Not all drugs that are available are necessarily prescribed – or legal. Illegal drugs can be divided into three main groups: stimulants, depressants, and mixed action drugs. Each type affects the brain, and therefore the body, in different ways.

Brain cells communicate information around the brain and body. Each cell is divided from its neighbor by a gap. Special chemicals called neurotransmitters jump this gap in order to transfer the information from one brain cell to another. This happens between the 10,000 million brain cells, with each transmission taking only a fraction of a second.

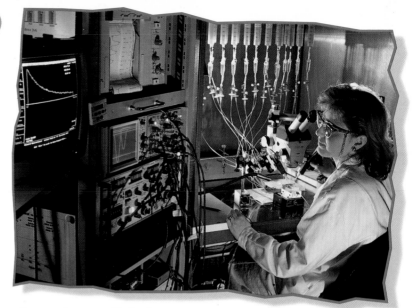

Drugs for medicinal use are carefully researched and tested under laboratory conditions.

RISKY BUSINESS

With all this information flying around, it must be quite difficult to make sure that it's all going to the right place at the right time.

Both medicinal and illegal drugs affect how the transmissions work. Before medicines are approved for people's use, they are carefully tested and the side effects researched as much as possible.

Illegal drugs do not have such precautions taken, however, and so each time a drug user takes an illegal drug, they are laying themselves open to a huge number of unknown risks.

WRONGFUL RELEASE

Stimulant drugs increase the release of the neurotransmitter chemicals, and so make the body's systems work harder and faster. This can make someone seem hyperactive. Depressants actually block the release of certain chemicals, and so can make the user seem depressed as the drug slows down the messages in the brain. And, as you would imagine, mixed action drugs produce both these effects.

Alcohol is a depressant. It confuses and can eventually kill neurons in the brain and dulls the body's senses and responses. It also affects your moods and emotions.

Young people are curious about life's experiences, so getting accurate information about the lifestyle choices you are making is a useful step. You need to know how drugs work and the effects they can have physically and mentally, to have accurate information on which to base your decisions about the life you choose to lead. It's not good enough being told to "Just say no." Knowing why to say no is much more important. Increasing self-esteem is another part of the equation. When you feel good about yourself, you're less likely to take foolish risks.

CASE STUDY

Diane's story

"It started when I was nine and a bridesmaid at a family wedding. My uncle Joe, who can't have been more than about twenty at the time, kept giving me drinks of sherry when my mom wasn't looking, and I really liked it. After that, I used to drink from the liquor cabinet in the front room when I was at home by myself. Sometimes during junior high school I went home for lunch and came back to school drunk. Some of the teachers used to look the other way, but eventually I was expelled and my mom threw me out of the house 'cause she didn't know what to do with me. To make a long story short, I lived on the streets for six years and became an alcoholic. I still am, although I haven't had a drink for over a year now."

UPDATE ON DIANE

Diane eventually accepted help from a social worker in a short-stay hostel and decided to start facing up to her problems instead of relying on alcohol to keep her confused and "out of it." She contacted Alcoholics Anonymous, started going to their meetings, and still does. Physically, Diane is still recovering from the effects that alcohol had on her body, which was starting to show signs of malnutrition. Fortunately she did not go on to develop diseases of the liver, pancreas, or kidneys, which are common in long-term alcoholics. Diane's physical dependence on alcohol left psychological scars as well, due to the life changes that becoming an alcoholic brought. She still has to come to terms with these events in her life.

Not only does drinking too much alcohol affect your body, but it can also play havoc with your moods and emotions.

"The reason that I don't drink is that I want to know when I'm having a good time."
Nancy, Lady Astor, 1879 – 1964

THE WHOLE STORY

Looking good and feeling good is much, much more than what you see in the mirror each morning, or what mood you're in when you wake up. The way you feel about yourself and the opportunities you give yourself make all the difference. Being aware of all your needs – your mind and body – seems quite a lot to think about, as well as remembering to take the dog for a walk, your library books back, your little brother to the babysitter's. But it's just a matter of getting into good habits – lifestyle habits – that suit you.

LOOKING AFTER THE WHOLE YOU

MULTIPLE CHOICE

Sometimes life can seem like a very complex system of multiple choices. There are often so many decisions to make about what you should do with your day, your week, your life, yourself. As you get older, the choices start to become more wide ranging. It's no longer a question of "what am I going to wear today" or "who shall I sit next to at lunch time," but more "what do I want to do when I leave school" or "should I try smoking that joint or not?"

THE LONG-TERM EFFECT

The choices you face as you get older start to influence your long-term future. Decisions you make may seem fine at the time, but later on you might wish you'd thought more about them.

> Oh, I'll just have this one. I don't want to make a fuss, or stand out as being different.

> My partner and I would really like to start a family. I want to give our baby the best start in life and I know that my smoking will affect its health before it's even born. I've smoked for ten years and I'm really having difficulty in giving it up. I don't even enjoy it that much...

THE ANSWER SHEET

Unlike multiple choice, there's not just one right answer to life's decisions. You have to decide what's right for you – and it doesn't have to be that hard. As you're faced with a decision, you don't have to be forced into giving your answer then and there, particularly if it's a big decision. (Don't take too long if your mom's asking what you want for lunch, though.) If it's a decision that could influence your future, then give yourself time to gather all the facts, talk to someone whose opinion you value, think about the consequences. And then decide. You'll know when you've made the right choice, because you'll feel relaxed about it and happy with yourself. And if you think you might have made a mistake and want to change your mind – well, you're allowed to do that, too.

PICK YOUR OWN!

So the crucial part of looking and feeling good is YOU (although family and friends are usually more than happy to lend a hand!). You can help to give yourself the best chances by making sure you look after your body and know your own mind. There are many options open to you. Which ones do you think you'll pick?

Habits can become lifetime choices - or lifetime choices can become habits.

LETTER FROM LIFE EDUCATION

Dear Friends:

The first Life Education Center was opened in Sydney, Australia, in 1979. Founded by the Rev. Ted Noffs, the Life Education program came about as a result of his many years of work with drug addicts and their families. Noffs realized that preventive education, beginning with children from the earliest possible age all the way into their teenage years, was the only long-term solution to drug abuse and other related social problems.

Life Education pioneered the use of technology in a "Classroom of the 21st Century," designed to show how drugs, including nicotine and alcohol, can destroy the delicate balance of human life. In every Life Education classroom, electronic displays show the major body systems, including the respiratory, nervous, digestive and immune systems. There is also a talking brain, a wondrous star ceiling, and Harold the Giraffe, Life Education's official mascot. Programs start in preschool and continue through high school.

Life Education also conducts parents' programs including violence prevention classes, and it has also begun to create interactive software for home and school computers.

There are Life Education Centers operating in seven countries (Thailand, the United States, the United Kingdom, New Zealand, Australia, Hong Kong, and New Guinea), and there is a Life Education home page on the Internet (the address is http://www.lec.org/).

If you would like to learn more about Life Education International contact us at one of the addresses listed below or, if you have a computer with a modem, you can write to Harold the Giraffe at Harold@lec.org and you'll find out that a giraffe can send E-mail!

Let's learn to live.

All of us at the Life Education Center.

Life Education, USA
149 Addison Ave
Elmhurst, IL
60126
Tel: 630 530 8999
Fax: 630 530 7241

Life Education, UK
20 Long Lane
London
EC1A 9HL
United Kingdom

Life Education,
Australia
PO Box 1671
Potts Point
NSW 2011
Australia

Life Education,
New Zealand
126 The Terrace
PO Box 10-769
Wellington
New Zealand

GLOSSARY

Anorexia nervosa An eating disorder in which a person deliberately starves him or herself in order to lose weight.

Bacteria Single-celled organisms, some of which cans cause illness if they get into the body.

Bulimia An eating disorder in which a person alternates binges or overeating with making him or herself sick in order not to put on any weight.

Calorie A unit of heat measurement used to express how much energy a food produces when it is used by the body.

Cholesterol A fatty substance that helps to digest certain foods. Our bodies make their own cholesterol, and we also get it from foods like butter, meat, and eggs. Too much cholesterol in the blood can lead to heart disease.

Gland An organ or group of cells that produces fluid that the body needs. The gland is generally named after the fluid that it produces, for example sweat or saliva glands.

Holistic Dealing with the whole person, both mind and body, rather than just individual parts.

Immunity The body's ability to fight off illness, infection and disease.

Metabolism The process in the body whereby chemical action allows nutrition, or nourishment within the body, to take place.

Microbes Tiny single-celled organisms (living structures) some of which cause diseases. However, many others do no harm and some living in the human body can actually help to keep it functioning properly.

Neuron A specialized cell that can receive messages and send them throughout the body. Neurons are found in the brain, spinal cord, and nerves.

Nicotine An addictive, poisonous chemical found in tobacco.

Puberty The time during which a child begins to develop into an adult, usually when he or she is between about 10 and 14 years old. Many important physical and emotional changes occur during puberty.

Viruses Tiny organisms that can only live and multiply inside other living cells. Viruses cause disease such as colds, measles, and AIDS.

Vitamins Nutrients essential for the body's health, but only needed in very small quantities.

FURTHER INFORMATION

The following organizations are useful sources of further information about topics covered in this book.

American Heart Association
7272 Greenville Avenue
Dallas, TX 75321
Telephone: 214-373-6300
Toll-free: 800-242-8721
Fax: 214-706-1341

American Lung Association
1740 Broadway
New York, NY 10019
Telephone: 212-315-8700
Fax 212-265-5642

President's Council on Physical Fitness and Sports
701 Pennsylvania Ave, NW
Suite 250
Washington, DC 20004
Telephone: 202-272-3421
Fax: 202-504-2064

TARGET
Helping Students Cope with Tobacco, Alcohol, and Other Drugs
11724 NW Plaza Circle
PO Box 20626
Kansas City, MO 64195
Telephone: 816-464-5400
Toll-free: 800-366-6667
Fax: 816-464-5571

INDEX